DATE DUE

DEMCO

ITALY

GALLERY BOOKS
An Imprint of W. H. Smith Publishers Inc.
112 Madison Avenue
New York City 10016

This edition first published in U.S.
in 1991 by Gallery Books,
an imprint of W.H. Smith Publishers, Inc.
112 Madison Avenue, New York, New York 10016

ISBN 0-8317-0263-X

Printed and bound in Spain

For rights information about the photographs in
this book please contact:

The Image Bank
111 Fifth Avenue, New York, NY 10003

Producer: Solomon M. Skolnick
Writer: Claudia Caruana
Design Concept: Lesley Ehlers
Designer: Ann-Louise Lipman
Editor: Joan E. Ratajack
Production: Valerie Zars
Photo Researcher: Edward Douglas
Assistant Photo Researcher: Robert V. Hale
Editorial Assistant: Carol Raguso

Title page: The ancients said all roads lead to Rome, and with good reason. For centuries, the eternal city and Italy have welcomed visitors. *Opposite:* Many Alpine Italian towns near the Austrian border are more Tyrolean in character than Italian.

Slightly larger than Arizona, Italy is a southern European country long on history and replete with culture. A boot-shaped peninsula jutting into the Mediterranean Sea, it is bordered on the northwest by France, on the north by Austria and Switzerland, and on the northeast by Yugoslavia. In addition to tiny islands in the adjacent Tyrrhenian Sea to the west, Italy lays claim to two larger Mediterranean islands, Sicily and Sardinia.

The Apennine Mountains vertically transverse Italy, and the majestic and towering Alps and Dolomites crown her to the north. It comes as no surprise, then, that the country is mountainous and rugged in most places, except for occasional breaks of coastal plains, such as the area south of Rome, the nation's capital, and the fertile Po Delta in the north.

Being at the crossroads of several countries, Italy is cosmopolitan and sophisticated, the home of sleek automobiles, modern architecture, and high fashion. It is opera, it is art, it is literature. But at the same time, Italy is rustic and traditional, with small, simple farms, outdoor markets, enduring pastoral views, and country churches.

What is known today as Italy was once a jumble of tiny empires, independent city-states, and papal jurisdictions. Visited by ancient Phoenicians and Greeks at the dawn of recorded history, Italy was also the birthplace of the Renaissance and such notables in the fields of art, music, literature, and science as Botticelli, Verdi, Boccaccio, and Galileo.

Little can compare with the glorious scenery of the majestic Dolomites, which are surrounded by dense pine forests and glimmering glacial lakes. Depending on the light, the Dolomites sometimes have a pink to reddish glow.

Without question, Italy is a country to explore and savor. The scenery is matchless. The people are warm and friendly. The famous cuisine, which varies from German-influenced cooking in the north to fresh seafood in the south, includes more than 100 varieties of pasta. 20 distinct regions divided into 95 provinces make up this democratic republic.

Lake Como, one of the more popular lakes in northern Italy, has been hosting visitors since Roman times, but most of the surrounding villas date from the seventeenth and eighteenth centuries. *Below:* Sirmione, a resort town located on a peninsula that juts into Lake Garda, is noted for its thirteenth-century castle surrounded by a moat.

Entirely surrounded by the Alps, the Aosta Valley is Italy's most mountainous region. The northeastern corner of the country, adjacent to the French and Swiss borders, is an important resort area. Breathtaking views of Mont Blanc, the Matterhorn, and the Gran Paradiso can be seen there. Numerous small Alpine lakes and several buildings from the Middle Ages, including the castles at Fénis and Issogne, dot the region.

Like the Aosta Valley, Piedmont is a "window on France" and it, too, is mountainous. Not unexpectedly, the area hosts several international ski centers, including Sestrière, Bardonecchia, and Sauze d'Oulx.

Turin, the regional capital, is a city that many say has a French accent, and it is often a gateway to France for Italians and tourists. There are many fine *piazzas* (open public squares usually surrounded by buildings) lined with baroque churches and palaces where residents and foreign visitors alike gather. Turin is no sleepy Alpine city. Often covered with smog, this city with many wide avenues is home to numerous manufacturing plants. The famous Shroud of Turin—the burial garment that supposedly covered the dying Christ—is kept in the city's cathedral. Interestingly, Turin also is home to the largest Egyptian Museum outside of Cairo.

South of Piedmont, along the coast, is Liguria. Facing the Tyrrhenian Sea, Genoa is the regional capital and Italy's largest port. Home to almost 200 churches, Genoa dates back to the fifteenth century and has excellent examples of baroque architecture. In

Above: The Neptune fountain in Trent stands in the Piazza Duomo surrounded by shops and cafés. *Right:* Trent is not only famous for the council held there from 1545 to 1563; it is also known for the painted facades on many of its buildings.

this region there are many seaside resorts, notably the towns of San Remo and Bordighera. There are also several medieval towers and castles near the Riviera di Ponente.

To the east of Piedmont, located on the major portion of the Po Valley, Lombardy has the distinction of being Italy's most populated region. Although there are tranquil lake districts here (Lake Maggiore, the lakes of Varese, Iseo, and Como, and the northern portion of Lake Garda), Lombardy is an economically active and rich region. Milan, the

Above: Portofino—which literally means "port of dolphins"—is a city on a horseshoe-shaped inlet on the Gulf of Genoa. *Left:* The Italian Riviera, with its Mediterranean climate and excellent beaches, is known throughout the world as a mecca for sunseekers.

Above: Paintings by Tintoretto, Van Dyck, and Bassano are spread throughout the upper gallery of Genoa's Royal Palace. *Below:* Ornate, rococo ceilings (left) dominate the interior of the palace. Designed by Bartolomeo Bianco and begun in 1650, subsequent alterations continued until about 1840.

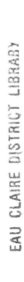

region's capital, is southern Europe's banking center. The city is also home to several top fashion houses and the world-renowned opera house, La Scala. The Galleria shopping mall in Houston was modeled on the Galleria Vittorio Emanuele, a shopping district of upscale boutiques and speciality shops in the heart of the city.

In Milan it is difficult to miss the *duomo*, the towering Gothic cathedral with 135 marble spires and 2,245 exterior statues. For this reason, many consider Lombardy the cradle of Romanesque architecture. The duomo, the third-largest cathedral in the world, can hold more than 20,000 worshipers. The duomo wasn't completed until 1897, although artisans began work in 1336. Inside, there are five huge aisles, massive pillars, and stained-glass windows that were made during the fifteenth and sixteenth centuries. On a clear day, visitors can see all of Milan as well as the Lombardy plains and the Alps from the cathedral's terraces.

Straddling the eastern portion of the Po Valley and part of the Dolomites, the Veneto region includes the rich Po Delta. It is also home to Venice, where most of the "streets" are waterways crossed by nearly 400 bridges. Called the "City of Canals," Venice is actually built on wooden piles on a lagoon three miles off the Italian coast.

This page, top to bottom: La Scala, Milan's famed neoclassical opera house, which can seat close to 3,000 people, was completed in 1778 and reconstructed after extensive bomb damage in World War II. The famous Galleria Vittorio Emanuele, a four-story glass-roofed arcade of posh boutiques and specialty shops, has been used as the model for many modern shopping malls. One of Milan's most notable landmarks, the Castello Sforzesco was converted to a series of museums in the last century and houses Michelangelo's *Rondanini Pietà,* the sculpture he was working on when he died.

Milan's Gothic duomo, with 35 marble spires and 2,245 exterior statues, is the third-largest cathedral in the world and can hold more than 30,000 worshipers. *Below:* The Castello's redbrick fortified walls have surrounded such famous court artists as da Vinci and Bramante.

Although there is a seawall against the Adriatic Sea, it is not unusual for the city to be flooded. Between November and April, there are extremely high tides, causing what is known as *acque alte*, "high water."

A famous congregating place for residents and visitors alike is the Piazza San Marco, which faces the huge Cathedral of Saint Mark. An adjacent trendy and upscale shopping district here is the reason for another name: "the expensive living room" of Venice. Nearby is the famous Doges' Palace, the home of the chief magistrate in the days when Venice was an independent republic. Also in the area is Harry's Bar, Ernest Hemingway's hangout while he lived in Italy and the watering hole for other literati.

Although many visitors envision *traghetti*, or gondolas, transporting them through Venice's canals, more common are the larger *vaporetti*, or motor-driven water buses. Using the *vaporetti*, two islands can be reached from Venice: Murano, where hand-blown glass is made and Lido, the setting for Thomas Mann's *Death in Venice*.

Trentino-Alto Adige is another mountainous province rich in rivers, waterfalls, lakes, glaciers, and coniferous forests that cover the Dolomite slopes. Many of the buildings and churches reflect the

Preceding pages: The tiny Venetian island of San Giorgio Maggiore is the site of a church of the same name that offers some of the best views of Venice. *This page, top to bottom:* 150 canals link the more than 100 islands that make up the city of Venice. The marble Rialto Bridge, one of three that span the Grand Canal, was completed in 1592 and is lined on both sides with shops. Galleried buildings line the San Marco Canal, which leads to the Grand Canal. *Opposite:* The campanile of St. Mark rises above the Piazza San Marco, the only piazza in Venice.

Above: St. Mark's Square has always been a meeting place for residents and visitors alike. *Below:* Honeymooners and pigeons (left) flock outside the lavish Basilica of St. Mark, which dominates the square. During Carnevale (center), the ten days leading up to Lent, Venetian merrymakers wearing costumes parade in the streets. The horses (right) that stand today outside the basilica are replicas of Roman bronzes from the second century.

architectural style of the Renaissance. Trent, the region's capital, is known as the site of the Council of Trent (1545), which started the Counter-Reformation.

Also in this region is Verona, an intact medieval city perhaps best remembered as the setting for Shakespeare's *Romeo and Juliet*. Thousands of visitors flock to this city annually to pay homage to the tragic lovers.

Bordering both Switzerland and Austria, Trentino-Alto Adige is the northernmost region in Italy. Frequently referred to as South Tyrol, many of its residents speak German, since the region was acquired from Austria after World War I. It is a region of castles and glorious Dolomite views, often red or pink depending on the time of day and lighting. Bolzano is its capital.

One of Italy's few flat regions, Friuli-Venezia Giulia includes the area between the Tagliamento River and the Adriatic coastline bordering Yugoslavia. For many years, the area was in dispute and was ruled by Yugoslavia. After World War II, the province returned to Italian rule. The regional capital is Trieste, the largest port in the Adriatic. There, and in the surrounding areas, are numerous ruins and archaeological sites, including a Roman theater which was excavated in 1938 and is estimated to date from the second century A.D.

Preceding page: The Bridge of Sighs is named for the sighs of prisoners who walked across it from the Doges' Palace, where they were sentenced, to the Palazzo delle Prigioni, where they were tortured or executed. *This page, top to bottom:* This large Roman arena in Verona, which dates from the first century A.D., is now the site of summer music festivals. The Villa di Poggio e Caiano, one of the Medici villas outside Florence, was converted to its palatial form for Lorenzo il Magnifico, a leading Florentine political figure, in the late 1400's. Bologna, a walled medieval city, is home to Europe's oldest university, the University of Bologna.

Above: The Palio—Sienna's famous horse race around the main square—was first held in 1656 and now takes place twice a year, on July 2 and August 16. *Below:* The marble quarries in Carrara (left) have been worked since Roman times; many of Michelangelo's statues were carved of marble from this source. Sienna's Palazzo Pubblico (right), with a 320-foot bell tower, is a Gothic palace built of stone and brick between 1297 and 1310.

Above: The Ponte Vecchio has been home to goldsmiths' and jewellers' shops since 1593. *Opposite:* The only medieval span over the Arno that was not destroyed by the Nazis in their retreat from Florence, the Ponte Vecchio dates from 1333.

Above: Lorenzo Ghiberti's bronze doors (left), which lead to the bapistry in Florence's Piazza San Giovanni, are so impressive that Michelangelo is said to have compared them to the gates of paradise. The Duomo (center), adjacent to the Baptistry, has a facade of pink, green, and white marble mined from three separate quarries. The Duomo (right), formally known as the Cathedral of Saint Maria del Fiore, was begun in 1294 but finishing touches were still being added in the nineteenth century. *Below:* Ghiberti's stunning east doors to the Baptistry contain dramatic scenes from the Old Testament.

This page: When the Duomo was first designed by di Cambio he included in his plans the world's largest dome, but no one knew how to build it. Filippo Bruneschelli eventually constructed the dome, which was later used as the model for the large dome on St. Peter's in Rome.

South of Friuli-Venezia Giulia, near the center of Italy, is Emilia-Romagna, a region between the Apennine Mountains and the Adriatic Sea. The capital is Bologna, which is a well-preserved medieval city and the home of the oldest university in Europe, the University of Bologna.

Important Roman ruins can be found near Ravenna, which was the capital of the Western Roman Empire in the fifth and sixth centuries A.D. In Ravenna is the Mausoleum of Galla Placidia, which was erected in the fifth century A.D. in the form of a Latin cross and is decorated with a variety of mosaics. Another famous, and more familiar person is buried nearby: Dante Alighieri, the author of the *Divine Comedy,* who died in 1321.

The Tuscany region, encircled by the Apennine Mountains, faces the Tyrrhenian Sea. From the coast, the small islands of the Tuscan archipelago can be seen.

Outside of Rome, this region may well be the best known and most visited area of Italy. One word says why: Florence. Although Charles Dickens called the streets of Florence "magnificently severe and gloomy," it is one of the world's most fascinating cities and the birthplace of the Italian language.

Over the centuries, Florence has been home to masterpieces and great works of art. The Renaissance blossomed here, and remnants of this remarkable period abound. Beautiful ecclesiastic architecture, including

Michelangelo's masterpiece, *David,* completed in 1504, graces the Academy Gallery in Florence. *Below:* The U-shaped Uffizi Gallery was originally designed by Vasari as an office complex for Cosimo I, but today it is one of the world's premier galleries and houses paintings by such masters as Botticelli, da Vinci, Michelangelo, and Titian.

The fabulous Boboli Gardens at the Pitti Palace, laid out in 1560, are filled with statuary, fountains, and terraces that offer stunning views of Florence. *Below:* Built for Luca Pitti in the mid-fifteenth century, the Pitti Palace later become home to the Medicis. Today it houses the Palatine Gallery and its collection of primarily sixteenth-century paintings.

Preceding page: Built between 1299 and 1314 as the seat of the city's republican government, the Palazzo Vecchio, with its 308-foot tower, is filled with frescoes and murals. *This page, above:* The Franciscan church of Santa Croce, begun in 1294, contains the tombs of such renowned men as Dante, Michelangelo, and Galileo. *Below:* Santa Maria Novella (left), a Dominican church, was begun in 1246, but its green and white geometric facade was designed by Leon Alberti in the mid-fifteenth century. This statue (right) belatedly honors Dante, who was exiled from Florence and died in Ravenna in 1321.

Giotto's bell tower, the Medici chapels, and the eight-sided Baptistry, grace the city. The Uffizi Palace and the Palatine Gallery at the Pitti Palace house sculptures and paintings from the Renaissance as well as from other periods. Also in the Pitti Palace are two special-interest museums: the Museum of the Costume and the Museum of the Carriages. Michelangelo's *David* is on view in the Academy Gallery, as are works by other artists, particularly Tuscans.

Outside Florence, incredible views can be taken in at the reserve of Monti dell'Eccellina, a nature preserve, and the island of Elba. The city of Pisa, a short distance away, is an ancient Roman naval base but is more famous for its tower, a campanile which leans about 14 feet off the perpendicular.

Another mountainous region on the Adriatic Sea, Marches, with its waterfalls, gorges, and streams, has invigorating scenery. Numerous Roman ruins in Fano and Urbisaglia, as well as examples of Romanesque architecture with a Byzantine influence, can be found in this region that was the birthplace of Raphael in Urbino and Rossini in Pésaro. The regional capital is Ancona, often a departure point to Greece and Yugoslavia.

Called the "green heart" of Italy, Umbria, a woody and mountainous region between Florence and Rome, is frequently overlooked by visitors. Italy's highest waterfall, the Falls of the Marmore, are here. Perugia, the region's capital now famous for chocolate and pasta production, is the site of the National Gallery of Umbria, which houses an impressive art collection representing the history of Umbrian painting. Near

The Piazza Grande in Arezzo, a Tuscan town, bursts into color the first Sunday in September with the *Giostra del Saraceno,* a costumed medieval joust.

Preceding page: A series of architects sought to correct the tilt of the Leaning Tower of Pisa over the 180 years of its construction, but they were unsuccessful. *This page, above:* Italy's leading arts festival (left), the Festival of Two Worlds, takes place every summer in the medieval town of Spoleto. The Church of San Rufino in Assisi (right) contains its original font, in which both Saint Francis and Saint Clare were baptized. *Below:* The Basilica of St. Francis, built in two levels over the crypt of the saint, contains Giotto's most famous frescoes, which celebrate St. Francis's life.

Above: The Palace of the Conservatori houses this bronze, *Lupa Capitolina*, a statue of the wolf suckling the mythical twins Remus and Romulus, who are said to have founded Rome in 753 B.C. *Opposite:* The Roman Forum, the heart of the Roman Empire, is in fragments today, but excavations begun in the nineteenth century continue to bring new insights into this amazing culture.

Above: Scattered towering columns (left) mark the remains of temples dedicated to various gods as well as to emperors. This statue (center) honors Julius Caesar, the Roman statesman famous for his conquest of Egypt. Although the forum was allowed to deteriorate during Rome's decline, some of the original temples (right) were consecrated as Christian churches. *Below:* The Forum of Trajan is now almost completely in decay, except for the semicircular market buildings. *Opposite:* Bas-reliefs on the Arch of Titus commemorate the sacking of Jerusalem.

Preceding page: The Colosseum, or Amphitheatrum Flavium, was completed in A.D. 80 and was inaugurated with 100 days of bloody games. *This page, right:* Part of the original four tiers remain on one side, but the statues that once graced the arches are long gone. *Below:* Although the floor of the Colosseum has been carted away, the tunnels through which animals were brought into the arena are still visible.

Perugia is Assisi, the home of Saint Francis, the patron saint of Italy.

Ancient, extinct volcanoes form the lakes in the hilly region of Latium. But the fascination for the region for both residents and visitors is its capital city: Rome.

Often called the "eternal city," no trip to Italy is complete without a visit to Rome. Legend has it that Rome was founded in 753 B.C. by the mythical twins Romulus and Remus. In keeping with the famous saying, all roads do seem to lead this city of stark contrasts— old, narrow streets and decrepit apartments in one section and charming piazzas and massive high-rises in another.

It is a city of history, art, and churches. The massive, baroque Church of the Gesù off the Piazza Venezia amazes worshippers and visitors with its painted ceiling whose artwork continues onto the pillars for a three-dimensional affect.

Rome's most glittering street, the Via Condotti, is a haven for shoppers from around the world. With such famous designer boutiques as Gucci, Bulgari, and Ferragamo, it can be expensive, but there are less costly pursuits. "People watching" at the nearby Caffè Greco, a 200-year-old establishment where notables such as Goethe, Byron, and Liszt enjoyed the passing scene is a popular pastime. Strolling in Rome's public gardens, such as the ones on the Janiculum Hill and at Villa Ada, Villa Borghese, Villa

This page, top to bottom: The Pantheon, Rome's most complete ancient structure, was completed in A.D. 127 and has amazed people for centuries with its perfectly symmetrical dome. The dome is 142 feet high and 142 wide, with a hole in the top 27 feet across which lets sun and light into the interior. This bust commemorates the emperor Constantine I, who converted Romans to Christianity.

Doria Pamphilj, and Villa Sciarra, which are remnants of parks created by wealthy families, is another favorite activity.

Just as in the movie *Three Coins in the Fountain,* people today continue to throw coins into the Trevi Fountain in the hope of returning to the city.

Most people make it a point to visit the Piazza Navona and the Spanish Steps in the evening when there are often free concerts or other events, as well as people taking the *passeggiata,* the customary early evening walk.

Almost all visitors to Rome stop to view the Forum, the center of public life in Rome's early republic. The enormous Pantheon is another well-preserved monument to early Rome's glory days, while the Colosseum, which dates from A.D. 80, has part of its original four tiers remaining. The Arch of Constantine near the Colosseum is an unusual arch—it features three interconnected arches and is studded with statues—that stands between the business district and the old city.

Partially formed by nature and partially dug by early Christians, Rome's many catacombs—there are at least 50—were used as a final resting place for the dead as well as a meeting place for the living. On the Via Appia Antica, the Catacombs of San Callisto have four levels and are more than 12 miles long. The tombs of several pontiffs from the third century and the Cubiculum of Saint Cecilia are within the complex of underground galleries. Another important group of catacombs are the nearby Catacombs of San Sebastiano.

Above: Angels by Bernini flank the Ponte Sant'Angelo, which crosses the Tiber. *Right:* The Castel Sant'Angelo, originally constructed in the second century A.D., later served as a fortress and is used today as a museum.

St. Peter's Basilica was originally conceived and designed by Bramante, but it was modified and completed by Carl Maderno over a century later. *Below:* Encircled by a quadruple file of Doric columns, St. Peter's Square contains an Egyptian obelisk and twin fountains, and can hold more than 300,000 people. *Opposite:* 140 statues of saints stand atop the columns surrounding St. Peter's Square.

Just as no visit to Italy is complete without a stop in Rome, no visit to Rome is complete without a stop at the Vatican. Established as an independent sovereign state by the Lateran Treaty of 1929, the 108-acre Vatican City, with the exception of Saint Peter's Square, is enclosed by high walls. This world's smallest state is home to approximately 1,000 people, including the pope.

Inside the walls of Vatican City are the basilica of Saint Peter, the Vatican Palace, the Vatican Gardens, the Vatican Library, and Belvedere Park.

Designed by Bernini, Saint Peter's Square is a curved piazza approximately 787 feet wide, encircled by a quadruple file of Doric columns. Within the square are two seventeenth-century fountains and an Egyptian obelisk that adorned Nero's circus.

On the place were Saint Peter was martyred is the basilica of Saint Peter. Reconstruction of the original church on the site, erected by Constantine in the fourth century, began in 1506 with Michelangelo creating the 436-foot-high dome and Maderno creating the face of the building. Inside are Michelangelo's *Pietá* and Bernini's *Baldacchino,* as well as other sculptures and a wealth of tombs. On the ceiling of the Sistine Chapel are Michelangelo's paintings of scenes from the Bible, and on the altar wall is his *Last Judgment.*

This page, top to bottom: The glory of the dome of St. Peter's, visible from nearly everywhere in Rome, is obscured in the square by the facade. The baroque facade of St. Peter's was completed by Maderno in 1614. The papal symbol of a triple crown surmounting crossed keys adorns a section of the colonnade that surrounds St. Peter's Square. *Opposite:* From this loggia above the central door to St. Peter's, the Pope gives his benediction to throngs gathered below on holy days.

Preceding page: The ceiling of the Sistine Chapel is covered with Michelangelo's paintings of scenes from the Bible, which took him four years to complete; *The Last Judgement* on the altar wall took him five years. *This page, above:* The apse in St. Peter's Cathedral is decorated with ornate carvings and paintings. *Below:* The soaring dome (left) of St. Peter's rises high above the baldachino. Bernini's 85-foot-high baldachino (right) supposedly marks the spot of the tomb of St. Peter.

The papal palace, home of the popes since 1377, consists of several buildings with more than 1,400 rooms, chapels, and galleries. The museums, the only part of the palace open to visitors, house the Vatican's collection of artifacts, which includes everything from illuminated manuscripts and Greek statues to furnishings and Egyptian sarcophagi and is estimated to cover more than four and one-half miles of displays.

Snuggled between the Apennine Mountains and Adriatic Sea, Abruzzi, in the middle of Italy, is home to the country's highest mountains, with peaks as high as 6,561 feet and a national park which is a haven for wolves, bears, and chamois, a kind of antelope. The terrain along the coast is steep and rugged. L'Aquila, the regional capital, is the site of an unusual 99-spouted fountain whose waters have sustained the residents of the city through famine, plague, and war.

Similar in terrain to neighboring Abruzzi, Molise also faces the Adriatic Sea, but north of the Gargano Promontory. Although it is the most recently created region, there are impressive ruins at Saepinum, Italy's best example of a Roman provincial town. Important Byzantine frescoes adorn the crypt of San Lorenzo in San Vincenzo al Volturno. In Campobasso, the Romanesque churches of San Bartolomeo and San Giorgio stand on a hill overlooking the town.

Above: The Vatican Museums comprise a series of palaces and galleries, built over centuries, which house the world's greatest collection of antiquities. *Left:* The Swiss Guards, the Pope's official bodyguards, are chosen from young, Roman Catholic, Swiss citizens.

Tourists throw coins into the ever-popular Trevi Fountain in the hope of returning to Rome. *Below:* The Piazzo Campidoglio, bordered on its north side by the Capitoline Museum, is one of the finest Renaissance squares.

Preceding page: The sixteenth-century church of Trinità dei Monti stands at the top of the Spanish Steps, a former gathering place of painters' models. *This page, right:* The Piazza Navona, a popular place for residents and visitors alike to take an evening walk, or *passegiata,* is flanked by expensive shops, cafés, and the church of Sant'Agnese. *Below:* The Fontana dei Fiumi in the Piazza Navona has four figures representing the Nile, Ganges, Danube, and Plate rivers.

The Vittorio Emanuele Monument, or Altar of the Nation, in the Piazza Venezia commemorates the unification of Italy in 1861. *Below:* The gardens at the Villa d'Este are filled with marvelous fountains and lush plantings.

Right: Marina Piccola is a little fishing village on the south shore of the Isle of Capri. *Below:* Capri, surrounded by the azure waters of the Gulf of Naples, has many grottos, or caves, the most famous of which is the Blue Grotto.

Campania encompasses some of Italy's finest coastlines. Facing the Tyrrhenian Sea and frequently referred to as the Amalfi coast, the gulfs of Naples and Salerno feature breathtaking views. From these vantage points, the tiny islands of Capri, Ischia, and Procida are visible. Naples, the regional capital, is one of Europe's most densely populated cities. It is often a starting point for explorations of three other important sites in this region: the ruins at Pompeii and Herculaneum, and Vesuvius, the volcano whose ashes and lava buried those cities centuries ago.

Apulia, the region at the heel of Italy's boot, has a dramatic coastline facing the Ionian and Adriatic Seas. A flat region in most places, there are high bluffs on some of the coastal areas. But visitors should not be surprised that there are sandy beaches here, too. Bari, the capital, is an important port and a ferry links the region to Yugoslavia and the Greek islands of Corfu and Igoumenítsa in the Adriatic Sea. Interesting churches in Bari include the eleventh-century Basilica of Saint Nicolas and a twelfth-century Romanesque cathedral, while the archaeology museum has important Neolithic and Bronze Age artifacts.

Further to the south, Brindisi, another port with ferries to Greece, is home to a column which dates from the first century B.C. and marks the end of the Via Appia, which linked the city to Rome in ancient times.

Below: Archaeologists believe this temple in Pompeii was dedicated to Isis, the goddess of fertility. *Opposite:* Pompeii has had more than its share of disasters—it was partially destroyed by an earthquake 13 years prior to the eruption of Mt. Vesuvius.

The instep of the Italian boot, Basilicata, has two coastlines—one at the center of the Gulf of Taranto in the Ionian Sea and a much smaller one in the Tyrrhenian Sea. The region is known for seaside resorts such as Maratea and Diamante. Basilicata is home to many archaeological ruins and excavation sites, including Greek ruins in Metaponto and ancient Roman ruins in Venosa, supposedly the home of the poet Horace.

In the most southwestern corner of Italy, or the bottom tip of the boot, is Calabria. Surrounded by the Tyrrhenian and Ionian Seas, it is a heavily forested and mountainous region with several picturesque lakes in the Sila Mountains. Its location made Calabria a crossroads for ancient Greeks and Phoenicians, and there are ongoing archaeological excavations, particularly at Locri. The National Museum in Reggio di Calabria houses artifacts from the Bronze and Iron ages, ancient Arabic art, and the Bronzes of Riace, bronze statues of warriors from the fifth century B.C.

Separated from Italy by the tiny Strait of Messina, Sicily, a former Greek colony, is a triangular, mountainous island. Palermo, the island's major city and regional capital, has both churches dating to the medieval age and ancient Roman ruins. Mt. Etna, the highest active volcano (10,902 feet) in Europe, is located in Sicily while a short ferry ride

This page, top to bottom: The House of the Great Fountain in Pompeii is named after this fountain in the house. The ornate wall paintings in Pompeii's Villa of the Mysteries depict scenes from a woman's initiation into a Dionysiac cult. Recent excavations have uncovered utensils and other domestic articles in surprisingly modern-looking houses. *Opposite:* Noted for its mosaic tile floors, the House of the Faun was the largest private house in Pompeii.

The mountainous Amalfi Coast on the southern part of the Sorrento peninsula is one of the world's most beautiful seaside regions. *Below:* Sorrento, a famous resort town on the Gulf of Naples, has been drawing visitors, including Ibsen, Nietzsche, and Wagner, for 200 years.

from Sicily to the Lipari Islands takes visitors to Stromboli, an active, smoldering volcano.

Sardinia, the second-largest island in the Mediterranean, is separated from France's island of Corsica by a narrow channel. Most people in Sardinia farm or fish for a living, but the mining of zinc, lead, and manganese also contributes to the regional economy. This mountainous island has occasional sandy beaches, particularly on the east coast, which is the site of the popular resort *Costa Smeralda*, the Emerald Coast. Underwater caves and grottoes, like the beaches, are sprinkled along the coast. The most famous of these is the Cave of the Sea Oxen, the last refuge of the rare Mediterranean monk seal.

From the heights of the Alps in the north to the coastal plains in the south, Italy embraces a vast and varied population. Fierce regional as well as family loyalties characterize many Italians, yet they are united by their pride in this distinctive and diverse land.

This page, top to bottom: Paestum is the site of the Temple of Neptune, which dates from approximately 450 B.C. *Trulli,* beehive-shaped houses often decorated with obscure symbols, are confined to a small section of the Puglia region; no one knows their significance. The church of Santa Maria dell'Isolla on the rocks above Tropea provides magnificent views of the Tyrrhenian Sea.

Above: The nude figures of the Pretoria Fountain in Palermo are still controversial after more than 300 years. *Below:* The Porta Felice (left) separates the city from the Bay of Palermo. This cathedral (right) in Palermo was consecrated in 1185, but its dome was not added until the eighteenth century. *Opposite:* The Temple of Concord in Agrigento dates from approximately 430 B.C. It was converted to a Christian church in the sixth century.

Preceding page: The temple of Castor and Pollux, with just these four Doric columns remaining, is composed of fragments from other buildings. *This page, above:* Catania's Roman Theater, which dates to the second century A.D., was built of lava on the site of an earlier Greek theater. *Below:* Segesta, an ancient city founded by Elymians, is the site of a well-preserved Greek temple and a small theater. *Overleaf:* Brilliant sunset drapes the recently reopened salt works at Trapani, Sicily.

Index of Photography

All photographs courtesy of The Image Bank, except where indicated *.